Welcome
Home

Perfect Peace

An introduction to your True Self

Perfect Peace

An introduction to Your Natural State Of Absolute Freedom As Unbounded Love: THIS is The Always Already Perfection That You Are.

From I Am To I Am With Love,

Charlie Hayes

Copyright © 2006-2009
Charles David Hayes

All rights reserved.

www.theeternalstate.org
non.duality@yahoo.com

ISBN 0-9766619-7-7
ISBN13 978-0-9766619-7-9

USA $15.95

For additional copies or volume discounts please contact Nonduality Expressions: 1-580-701-4793

Sri Nisargadatta Maharaj

This book is, in a manner of speaking, a blessing from The Guru of Gurus - Sri Nisargadatta Maharaj - the Bombay Sage whose talks with seekers are on record in several books, most notably "I Am That) (Acorn Press.) Sri Nisargadatta is currently appearing presently as the Totality Of Creation - *and* arises as Source of all the great Self-Expressions of Teachers Of What Is - out of timeless being, in the tradition of the Navnath Sampradaya.

Sri Ramana Maharshi

Much Grace flows to us from Sri Ramana Maharshi - whose pointing to ASKING "Who Am I?" (and accepting NO answer!) can provide a final push into Self-Realization.

Sri Ramana was my first Guru. Jaya Jaya Bhagavan Sri Ramana!

John Wheeler

&

"Sailor" Bob Adamson

Two most unlikely Sages - in the lineage of Sri Nisargadatta Maharaj - are my dear Teacher-Friends John Wheeler of California and "Sailor" Bob Adamson of Melbourne, Australia. John is a Bright Burning Flame of the Real. Good On Ya, Bob. Thanks, John.

"Perfect Peace"
Is Dedicated To

*Charles Edward, Rachel,
and Sarah Hayes*

The Future is
in good hands.

Table of Contents

INTRODUCTION: THE BEING OF ALL BEINGS...........14

ONE: THE AMAZING JOURNEY...............................26

TWO: PRESENCE-AWARENESS 32

THREE: DREAMS OR REALITY? 36

FOUR: THE MYTH OF ENLIGHTENMENT...................42

FIVE: THE BASICS 50

SIX: BE NOTHING, KNOW NOTHING.......................60

SEVEN: WHAT WORKS?..64

EIGHT: WHO OR WHAT ARE YOU?.........................68

NINE: WHAT YOU ARE NOT...................................74

TEN: ANY WHEN BUT NOW?..................................80

ELEVEN: SUFFERING ENDS NOW..........................86

TWELVE: SUFFERING IS ABOUT A "ME".................92

THIRTEEN: SUFFERING IS DISTINCT FROM PAIN.....96

FOURTEEN: IS ANYTHING NOT "IT?".................102

FIFTEEN: END GAME..106

SIXTEEN: AN EGO'S LAST STAND 108

SEVENTEEN: BE STILL & KNOW, I AM..................114

EIGHTEEN: LOOKING FOR THE KEYS....................116

NINETEEN: WHAT AM I MISSING?........................118

TWENTY: SELF CLEARS ITS SELF........................126

TWENTY-ONE: WHAT NEVER CHANGES?...............134

TWENTY-TWO: IN THE END..................................136

APPENDIX ONE: RAMANA....................................138

APPENDIX TWO: NAVNATH SAMPRADAYA.............140

APPENDIX THREE: GURUMAYI'S TRADITION.........142

ABOUT THE AUTHOR...144

NO WAY OUT..154

"The flame of love is not different from you; it is you. It isn't that love is there and you are here. You and love are one and the same."

- Gurumayi Chidvilasananda

Perfect Peace

An introduction to your True Self

Love Is The Great Mystery

Love appears as love and hate - equally.
Love appears as compassion and fear - equally.

This Love is The Great Mystery.

It cannot be held by you. It IS You - with all your
loving and hating, and all your pride and shame -
as you are, as you are not
You Are This Love.

Love Is All There Is.

Impossible to know.

IMPOSSIBLE NOT TO BE.

Being Love Is Inescapably Yours.

"Ishan"

Introduction: The Being of All Beings

This short book is a distillation of two longer Self-Expressions, the books *"From I Am to I Am, with Love,"* and "*Life After Death.*" This one is both a useful and handy review of the basic pointers set forth in those two texts <u>and</u> a concise exploration into Nonduality and Eternal Being - and it also contains material not to be found in the first two books.

These Works are offered as a sharing of the Timeless Being of Eternal Peace that is the True Nature of the appearing world and the "person" who seeks that "Peace that passeth understanding." They are for those seekers of peace that find themselves drawn to the authentic pointing to what is real, and what is not, via the Teachings of Advaita Nonduality. Most who are drawn to these Teachings have tried many paths, to no avail.

Here is the opportunity and invitation to step OFF the path and realize That which you already are - Pure Unbounded Love - The True Self of All.

A Meeting with Sri Nisargadatta

This strange and wonderful event occurred as I was out walking - an odd looking, somewhat bent over old man was suddenly noticed coming toward me as I was walking along inwardly humming a Ramana bhajan - "om namo bhagavate sri ramanaya" - to myself, happily striding along in a beautiful crisp California winter morning.

The sky blue as clarity can be - the slight breeze - the hum of traffic - all wondrous Being - and then . . .

The man came closer, looking down at the ground, ambling along- a cigarette in a gnarled hand - and as we came near I looked at him and said, "heya!"

Bang!

He look up and straight at me – dead on– and with his cigarette (I'd swear it was one of those little Indian "beedies") poised for a puff, grinned and met my eyes – it was Nisargadatta. Really – in my direct experience – it was He.

For a stunned moment we stared into infinity – One Essence meeting on a cool morning under a canopy of blue and green – skies and trees – all was stopped and all was Loving being that is all!

Bang!

The moment passed, the man grinned again, not a single word uttered – none were needed – then he laughed out loud, and sauntered off.

Darshan!

I stood stock still. My brain knew it was impossible that Nisargadatta had "reincarnated" this moment. But my Heart knew better – there was and is no doubt that this was "Darshan" of the great

Master himself. *(Darshan: A blessing conferred by seeing or touching a great or holy person.)*

The sage Bhagavan Nityananda of Ganeshpuri has - as the stories go - appeared in similar ways to this to devotees - and I was always a bit skeptical whether the stories were actually true.

But having this experience really erased all doubts, leaving in the wake of that experience a clear and total knowing that, in Divine Timeless Being, ANYTHING IS POSSIBLE. And in Truth - I Am That I Am - non-conceptual Awareness - Simply - Being. Just as Nisargadatta IS, so I AM.

Anything Is Possible -
    and that means - anything!

As the man walked away I pranamed, hands folded in respect, love pouring out all around.

When I finished my walk around the block he was nowhere to be seen. But and for the next hour I *experienced* seeing God in every blade of grass.

His Divine Presence remains as the most palpable sense of aliveness and Love imaginable (or really – Unimaginable!) - as the Natural Stateless State of Being - in Perfect Peace.

Being Is All There Is

THIS is Perfect Peace.

How This Book Came About

All there is, IS Perfect Peace. But not for the "person" ... for no one.

This Peace appears to itself (so to speak) in the dream of living as the Absence of the "person."

The waking-sleepwalking dream of "life" is seen <u>as</u> a dream, appearing in the Peace of this always

Presencing ... right here right now. The game of hide and seek has ended. Allee Allee in free!

Here and Now, Life is, as a metaphor, like a lucid dream. Endless peace alone is.

This is a book for those who are fed up with "spiritual seeking" and "psychological suffering" ... depression, anxiety, insecurity, fearfulness, anger... all of which make life miserable for those afflicted by these things. I know. I suffered from depression and bipolar disorder for 65 years. *(Yes, 65 years, from the age of five. The organism is now nearly 73 years old.)*

I was often suicidal, and medications didn't work. I would pray often to die.

While I feel that little story of "me" is of no real value in the grand scheme of things (not that there actually IS any "grand scheme of things!") some who still believe they are a suffering phantom character may find it useful ... just understand, I AM NOT THE STORY. Neither are YOU!

The best way to describe ANY "story of a person" would be in the words of Shakespeare: "A tale told by an idiot, filled with sound and fury, signifying ... nothing."

Sing along ...
"Row, Row, Row your Boat,
   Gently Down the Stream
     Merrily, Merrily, Merrily, Merrily,
       Life is But a Dream."

Oneness HerSelf designed this text to give you the absolute bare essentials, without dogma or "spiritual" trappings. Just the facts ... what is real and what is not real ... and the simplicity of the (apparent) cause, and cure, of psychological suffering.

Nobody Home

I did NOT "become enlightened." There is no such thing as an "enlightened person!" Nor is there any BODY that gets enlightened: The body is made up of the elements ... Water, air, fire (98.6 degrees of that), earth (food grows there and feeds the body) etc ... That body is meat. And, there is NO "enlightened "MEAT."

What happens is, in a way, nothing. That is to say, what happens is the one who was suffering is seen to be a phantom, an imaginary character, no more substantial than in idea in mind, a thought. And this thought has no power, no free will, and no volition, is uncaused and causes nothing. It is just an appearance, a will o' the wisp, the phantom of the soap opera called "my" life ... all nothing but story. When the storyteller is seen to be false the whole story is seen to be nothing but a bunch of thoughts, like clouds in an empty sky.

So long as the play, the dream, seems real, for the seeker, with some pointing to what is actually REAL, AND some pointing out what is NOT REAL, the suffering can end. I was in terrible shape when I encountered these pointers. The end of suffering did not happen overnight. There were physical issues to deal with as well as the mental despair. But ultimately, the pointers sink in and the clarity and freedom opens sort of from the inside out. You are invited with love, to work with the pointers. And play with the concepts. But do NOT believe any of what you read. Knowing your True Nature is NOT a matter of belief! It is a direct non-conceptual knowingness that is plain and simple, and unfiltered by mental constructs ... including the core constructs called "Me-Myself-I-Mine."

The bottom line is simplicity itself: Right here, right now, you know that you are. You exist and you are aware that you exist. That is it ... what you have sought is already here, clear and present.

That Thou Art.

But don't take anyone's word for anything ... DO the homework, and see for yourself: You are already free. You are already abiding as natural stillness, in silence, as peace. Discover this for yourself. Then your own True Nature will (so to speak) "say" in silence, softly, Welcome Home, dearly beloved. Welcome Home.

As Sri Nisargadatta Maharaj said: "*Your own [True] Self is your ultimate teacher (sat-guru). The outer teacher (guru) is merely a milestone. It is only your inner teacher that will walk with you to the goal, for it is the goal.*"

Caveat Emptor

This book is a description of an unfolding that happens. The words are dead ... life is where YOU are right here, and right now. Period.

<u>You *are* the Peace that you seek.</u>

A reader says: "*Thanks very much for your e-book "Perfect Peace." It certainly cleared up a lot of doubts, in fact it wiped me out - all there is left is clarity - Just this clear space in which everything appears. I can't say what it is or who it is - I only know that it is. There's no difference, no separation - except in thoughts. And those thoughts come and go in this Presence/Awareness. Thanks again.*"

~ ~ ~

From the Unreal to the Real

The Jewel Of Discriminating Awareness Shining Here Points to Your Perfect Peace

Perfect Peace

"*I am the nature of Pure Consciousness. I am always the same to beings, one alone; [I am] the highest Brahman, which, like the sky, is all-pervading, imperishable, auspicious, uninterrupted, undivided and devoid of action. I do not belong to anything since I am free from attachment. I am the highest Brahman... ever-shining, unborn, one alone, imperishable, stainless, all-pervading, and nondual-That am I, and I am forever released.*"

- Adi Shankara, *The Upadesasahasri*

And SO Dear Reader, are YOU. This Is Pointing to YOUR True Nature. Be That and Nothing Else.

One: The Amazing Journey

Come Back to Timeless Being ... The Home You Never Left. The journey of Self-discovery is the most wonderful, frightening, and exciting journey in this dream of life and living!

This is a book for seekers. If you have been on a spiritual quest, whether for 30 years or 30 days, this book is designed as a communication from your True Nature direct to That which knows that you ARE what you seek: That simple "I Am", that you are in truth, That which is universal and unbounded.

There is a radical and revolutionary message contained in the words and spaces of this book, AND there is an energy-Intelligence that is at the heart of the message ... a silent throb of pure Consciousness that communicates outside of time and space. That Consciousness ... Timeless Being ... Perfect Peace ... has been hiding in plain sight ... right before your very eyes. This book, when read with trust and openness, can reveal that which is Always So as your authentic True Nature ... directly, here and now.

"To know the always so is to be illumined."

- Lao Tzu

There is nothing missing in what you truly are. You need not change, or evolve, or purify, or self inquire, or meditate, to BE what you already are. In fact, all such attempts to "get to" what you are will naturally fail. Because you already ARE what IS ... perfect, stainless, being-awareness, self-shining and ever fresh!

There is only Wholeness, Unicity, Beingness ... arising as an impersonal knowing that what you are has never been lacking in any way.

Perfect Peace

The essence of Life that is at the heart of all matter, the simple knowingness, "Non-Conceptual, Impersonal Existence Is, and I Am That," is absolutely undeniable ... and inexpressible. *The words only point to That which cannot be known by the mind.*

Right NOW you ALREADY ARE Your True Nature. What were the ancients, and the sages, referring to as our REAL Self? It is Just This:

You exist and you are aware. What you sought and needed to know was only ever this. You are this Non-Dual Presence-Awareness... simply Being. The direct knowing of Being this is the Peace that Passeth Understanding.

Stop.

Around now, you might ask, "OK, but what about suffering? I have heard some teachers say that suffering is Oneness and nothing can be done about it because there is no person therefore suffering must endure."

The idea that suffering is inevitable comes out of the notion that who we are is totally powerless. But in actual fact what we truly are IS ALL power, ALL knowingness, ALL Presence. Omnipotence, Omnipresence, Omniscience. That Source of ALL life and the entire manifestation is what we REALLY are ... and one of the worst things the mind does is limit that with words!

This is the grand paradox: There is NO such thing as a separate person in the organism apart from this Omnipotence, Omniscience and Omnipresence. AND the innate intelligence-energy that keeps the stars in perfect order can certainly come to bear on human suffering. Now hear this: Suffering Is Optional! Keep it if you like, but if you are interested in living free of that unnecessary evil keep reading and looking within, with your OWN natural intelligence (NOT the mind; the answer is not in your thinking mind!)

By the way what to do with a paradox? Don't try to resolve it ... that will make the mind crazy. Sit with it like a brick in your lap. Just BE with it. And put it to inquiry: Who thinks this is "true" and that is "false?" Neither are "the truth. NO concept is "the truth!" Words only point. Try to quench your thirst with only the WORD "water!" The menu is not the meal ... the map is not the territory.

Here is a central pointer toward the end of suffering: ALL suffering is based on the idea of a separate "me" ... a person in the machine. But is there any such thing?

Apart from a thought of an "I" is there any actual entity anywhere in there? For "me", looking, looking like my life depended on it (because it did!), was the key. I absolutely cannot find a "me" or an "I" or a "myself" ... it is absent.

But this cannot be accepted or believed. IT HAS TO BEEN SEEN through a no holds barred investigation. Do or die.

Perfect Peace

"There is Nothing That Is Not Shiva."

- Nondual Kashmir Shaivism

(Note: Shiva is another word for Being - as are Consciousness, Totality, Tao, God, No Thing, Cognizing Emptiness, and Presence-Awareness. Pick the one that warms your heart and discard the rest.)

Two: Presence-Awareness (is Perfect Peace)

There is a huge paradox in all this. In truth there is no person. It is not that there is nothing to be done; it is that there IS no one to do or not do anything. But so long as we do not live in and as that Understanding, then looking needs to happen. It is sort of like this: So long as you think you are the "doer" of actions, take the actions of looking within, doing the inquiry. What do you have to lose? Your suffering.

So, there is no one; AND as long as it seems there is someone, there is suffering, and the investigation needs to happen. THEN, once the gateless gate has been passed, then it is seen, by no one, that there never was a dream or a separate character or any investigation. And life flows simply and effortlessly ... for no one. As it always did. But now it is realized.

All is just happening in this that you are ... awareness-presence.

The search... and the suffering ... DOES end. But NOT because someone finds something. It is simply seen that there is nothing to find, and no one to find it. You already are That which is sought.

As we go on we will delve into these points in a variety of ways. Rather than try to figure out what is right or wrong about what's being said, look onto the space of your own natural awareness, and see what you see. What you discover might just surprise ... and delight ... you.

To paraphrase the sage Sri Nisargadatta Maharaj, once you realize, no kidding, that nothing can trouble you but your own imagination, you are free in and as your self-shining, unbounded, True Nature.

Nothing in this book is "the truth."

What does that mean? Simply this: All words are concepts, language, letters; at bottom just sounds. Is the sound in your ears of "water" ever going to quench your thirst? No. The word water, no matter how loudly or lovingly said, will never BE water. The word water is a representation of a substance known to be clear, wet, and thirst-quenching.

Similarly, the concepts in this book represent certain "spaces" which cannot be captured by concepts or sounds or pictures ... because the SPACE is BEYOND all such forms and formulations.

So look where the concepts point, NOT taking the concept to be the Real.

The truth cannot be captured by words and images.

Perfect Peace

*You find that you cannot end
he search and attain what you seek.*

Ask within - who cannot end the search?

And the search ends - here.

Three: Dreams Or Reality?

Who, or what, awakens a dream character from the dream at night? Can that character know he is a dreamed character? No. Only the body-mind dreamer can awaken and see that it was in fact only a dream, not real. And that the subject-character and all the objects ... scenery, other characters etc ... were never actually real at all. It only seems real to a dreamed character, never to the body-mind dreamer.

Who Wakes Up?

So who awakens the "person" to the realization that what he thinks of as life is actually only a dream, exactly like the sleeping-dream, except with more seeming persistence and solidity? Can a person ... a dreamed character arising in the Self ... the Dreamer in this metaphor ... ever wake itself up?

Upon awakening in the morning, perhaps a vivid dream is remembered ... sometimes even with fondness for the characters. (I recall a number of such dreams where there were wonderful lovers!) But there is no delusion about these characters having any substance or existence whatsoever.

I also recall a series of night dreams where there was a seeming continuity ... some character from previous dreams reappeared, and all sorts of prior dream-events were remembered, giving seeming continuity to a story that seemed real and alive. But only to the "me" in that dream.

This waking dream is precisely the same with the added dimensions of apparent persistence and solid sensible continuity. This appearance, called Maya in the East, is the magical dark woolen veil of the Dreamer pulling the wool over the eyes of its own True Nature, so to say. Why? It just happens. No one can answer why (though many try, doomed to the ultimate realization that it is a mystery of magnificent proportions.)

In Reality there is no dreamed character. How could there be? The "you" that you think you are blows totally away in the seeing that all there IS, is the Dreamer ... the Self ... and nothing else has any actual solidity or persistence, any more than the night-dream does. The search for joy and peace, or liberation, is all over then.

The play continues as long as the organism lives, but there is no possibility that once the Dreamer has awakened to its Self so to speak, that any belief that all of this play is real and separate from the Dreamer can be sustained. Even if a delusion arises it is quickly seen as what it is by the Dreamer as insubstantial. And Poof. It's gone. (Again, 'so to speak;' the Dreamer is not separate from what is seen; words always fail!)

The pointer is that all efforts by a dream character to wake himself or herself to what REALLY IS cannot possibly succeed, any more that a nighttime dream-person can satisfy an urge to empty the bladder by peeing into a dream toilet. (I have had the experience of attempting that as a dreamed character many times; fortunately the body-mind wakes up and shuffles off to the bathroom just in time to avoid ruining the bed sheets!)

The dream-reality at night is only real to the dreamed character, never to the body-mind dreamer.

The bigger longer more seemingly connected event-by-event called the "waking state" is exactly the same only much more elaborate. That's all.

When the Dreamer wakes her Self to her Self, then it becomes a celebration of aliveness, but not for the person. There is no enlightened meat. Only the Dreamer ... Oneness, The Self, True-Nature, whatever concept you like, can know that there never was a dream.

The Dreamer Inquires — Who Am I?

The Dreamer HerSelf arises in thought as Self Inquiry. Asking the last question, the one that counts, dissolving Her dream ... Who Am I? We think <u>we</u> do it. And so it does seem! The belief that we cannot do it is more leads to more suffering by far, than the temporary belief that we can, in the so-called process.

In fact, we do nothing. Doing happens. Including for some fortunate patterns, Inquiry. Call it Grace, or any other label ... it is simply Self arising to see Self, One becoming many, folding back into One ... the Dream of the Source. Great sport! Loving to be, living as all that is, yet aloof in way. Paradox.

Beautiful stuff, this apparent creation. Literally incomprehensible in magnitude. Awe and humility are inevitable when this Magnificence arises and there is no one to see it. Loving to be. Just that, and all is well.

Wakey wakey.

Perfect Peace

Ponder for a while . . .

You have been invited to meet The Friend.

No one can resist a Divine Invitation.
That narrows down all our choices
to just two:
We can come to God
Dressed for Dancing
Or
To be carried on a stretcher
to God's ward.

- Hafiz

Four: The Myth of Enlightenment

So you are a seeker, right? You seek the holy grail ... absolute permanent happiness, the bliss of a thousand orgasms, the light of a thousand suns, the eternal Light, Brahman, God Consciousness ... or whatever other label piqued your fancy that made you say, Aha! Enlightenment! "I want THAT." And made you a seeker.

A note here about "being a seeker:" do you think YOU chose to put yourself through the torture of being a seeker? Think again! A thought arose, a book showed up, a Maharishi appeared on a TV show, he was so charming in his white dress and all his devotees loved him so ... something happened, and something took hold of you, and as one sage put it,

"Your head went into the tiger's mouth." And when the tiger bites off your head, nobody knows. But if you are like I was, you pray that the tiger bites down and ends the suffering. Because, make no mistake, seeking God or whatever IS pure suffering.

Now you are (let's be honest!) hoping THIS book will "Do It for Me." Right? I know the feeling ... been there done that got the t-shirts (a whole bunch of them.) I have good news and bad news. The bad news is, there is NO such "personal state" as enlightenment that you can ever attain.

The good news is, there is NO such "personal state" as enlightenment that you can ever attain. So you can quit seeking, right?

Well, maybe not! As you go through this little guide to get from the unreal to the real, you will with any luck at all discover that the whole issue is moot, because Ta Da there ain't any you to get enlightened! And all there is already IS the Real.

Perfect Peace

See, the REALLY good news is, all there already is, is "enlightenment" and you are already that. It's just that "YOU" cannot OWN THAT ... because THAT is the absence of the one who wants to own That which is the Real Nature of That.

So what to do? Read the book, try looking in the ways suggested, and take what you get. Then what you may discover is The Cosmic Joke: There is no one who needs to find God or Source, because the One who is looking IS ALREADY Source.

Listen up: You ARE what you seek. YOU ARE Oneness. Perfect Peace. Ultimately there is no separate "you!" All there is, is Being - appearing as you and other than you.

YOU ARE "The Open Secret," as Wei Wu Wei dubbed This.

As you are, you are Being.

As you are not, you are Being.

Contradictions appear. Being is ALL.

There is a notion, quite popular in "spiritual" circles, that the "Great Beings" or "Enlightened Masters" are somehow special, and have had miraculous powers bestowed upon them by "Grace" or some other nonsense. Look: There are NO enlightened PEOPLE. There is no enlightened "MEAT." The body-mind organism is a machine. No more special than a duck, or a tree!

When there is "Self Realization" then there is no person who owns that. There is simply LIFE living itself through that vast billions of objects, some sentient, some not... in a marvelous phantasmagoria, a profound and brilliant display of light, color, sound, silence, movement, stillness ... all appearing right before your eyes in a stunning overload of stimuli that seemingly masks the illusory dreamlike nature of the whole play.

It's All the Play of Consciousness.

Unbelievable? Yes. As a belief these word are useless. Look at what the words point to though, and you may see clearly what is Real ... and what is not.

For one through whom the realization has arisen and ripened, anything is possible; anything may arise in the Aliveness of the present moment of timeless being, and subside.

A popular Myth:

Enlightened beings are never angry

Reality: The body mind organism has its functioning in the Totality of all that is. This includes "programming" so to speak ... the essential DNA and subsequent conditioning ... and if the appropriate stimulus arrives, the response could be anger or any other emotion. So it would be good to drop the idea that anger will never arise. It DOES ... but for no one. (That will make more sense later!)

This idealized picture of some perfect Master in white smiling beatifically down on his "flock" can be easily dispelled with a little imagination: Imagine you are able to follow one of these blokes around hour after hour. Sooner or later he will have to eat, sleep, and visit the rest room. Guaranteed! Then, you may see through the charade and realize, hey, he is just like me. The Guru act is all a dog and pony show! And it keeps us mesmerized, and apparently "separate" from The Great Master Guru who seemed to be SO much holier than we are.

Then there is the ever-popular myth of "Someday." You know this one, right? "Someday I will realize my true nature. One more seminar, one more book (maybe THIS one!) or one more Satsang ... one more retreat and THEN "I will get It" ... the big elusive IT! Someday.

Lookit: Haven't you noticed, SOMEDAY NEVER COMES!? Where is the future right now, right here? What is this future? Without language, IS there any such thing? Stop and look. Your life ... your aliveness ... does it happen someday?? Or right now? Have a look ... not thinking about it, just sit in your own aliveness and look.

Where is someday?

Absent.

Yet the myth persists in the mental story, imagined to be "real," that "I" will "Get It" "Someday." See through this. Then consider the possibility that the Self you seek is already attained here and now. Presently, livingness IS. That livingness, that experiencing, IS what you are. This book provides pointers toward the natural seeing of this for yourself. Don't skip over them... really USE them to realize that you are already free, whole, complete ... you are the essence of love and happiness, naturally connected to all that is ... because you ARE all that is.

Understand this, stop and really GET this right now:

Psychological Suffering is Optional.
Psychological Suffering is Unreal.
Psychological Suffering is NOT, in Reality.
Let the suffering end here and now.

*The Universal Self is in the individual self.
Real Liberation is to know the subtle in the gross,
the unity in diversity,
the similarity in differences,
the Truth in untruth,
the Light in darkness
the Life in death.*

THIS is Real Liberation.

- Sri Bhagavan Nityananda of Ganeshpuri

Five: The Basics

The Core seeing is contained in this chapter. There will be more and different expressions of it, and other pages to facilitate a kind of looking and seeing, but this chapter has what you need to know and see and imbibe for your suffering, and seeking, to come to a halt! The basics. There are just TWO POINTS to imbibe. It is very simple!

1. Awareness is ever-present; that's what you ARE. (This is NON-conceptual Awareness-Presence ... not 'someone's awareness of something.' I call THAT manifest functioning, 'Consciousness.')

2. The separate "person" is a myth; that's what you are NOT. On investigation (often but not always) this seen ... by no one.

This awareness is obviously present at all times. It is non-conceptual; it is just the natural knowing of your actual ever present BEING.

Ultimately my concept is, Freedom ... Liberation ... whatever label you like ... is UNCAUSED. There is no "free" or "liberated" person. THAT is an oxymoron. As you will hear many times, if the dream has unfolded such that you find yourself bitten by this non-duality bug, as I was.

In short: What you are, IS ... Awareness, Presence, the knowing that you are, you exist ... translated by the mind into the thought I Am. And what you are NOT is a separate entity, an "I" in a world of "other."

This can be seen easily when there is no one looking. Paradox? Yep.

Perfect Peace

This game is not to be played by "the individual" ... because, there isn't one. How can you play if you don't exist as a player? Read on, and allow the game to come to you as best you can... because once these two pointers are seen and imbibed the game of separation – and suffering – is over. Done. Finished. So let's play!

Are you seeking, and suffering?

That suffering can end, right now. No kidding.

What ultimately works is simply looking at what is real and what is not ... which you can do right now... and the search can end, right here, right now! Take your time with this. There is no rush ... in fact to hurry this looking could get in the way. Be gentle and consistent, as best you can.

Do you Exist?

Right now: Check in to your own sense of awareness, and see the natural knowing that you exist and are aware, right now: Do you doubt that you exist? And that you are aware? No one can deny the fact of his or her own existence. This simple always present Awareness of Being IS what has been sought. It is so simple.... That is always here now, was never missing, just overlooked.

Who am I? Where is that I?
When was "I" born?

Now, have a look, to see if there is really a separate "me" that can suffer ... is there a "person" in the organism? Isn't "me" just a *thought*? Who is thinking? Who is looking? Some investigation reveals that the separate person is completely non-existent. Seeing the unreal nature of the "me" allows for an immediate end to psychological suffering.

When was the "me" born!?

If you ask "when was I born" the answer might likely be "on such and such a date - the organism's moment of appearing as a body-mind separate from other body-minds and the world.

That is hearsay! Objection! The lawyer said. Hearsay. Unverifiable!

Don't assume facts not in PRESENT EVIDENCE. That is the false entity, proclaiming itself to be real. Nothing more.

With some looking, it can be seen that awareness is present and the separate person is absent. *Seeing this is not a mental construct. The answer is NOT in the mind!* It is a clear knowing without words or anything else. It just IS. Inescapable and undeniable.

Presence-Awareness, Just This and nothing else.

You ARE NOT That ... THAT is BEING. And that's That. It's NOT that "you" are Being.

It is That ALL THERE IS, IS BEING. Chew on that!

BUT: Right here, right now, you know that you are. You can say, I Am That. Awareness. And whether you say that or not you are still that! You exist and you are aware that you exist. That is it ... what you have sought is already here, clear and present. That Thou Art. Do you doubt that? Fine. Just see that any doubt arises right here within that self-same awareness that you are.

Then what is UNREAL? What is the source and cause of psychological suffering?

The false sense of being a separate person, an "entity," is the root of all suffering. See through that false self-center and the plug is pulled on suffering once and for good.

Right NOW ... you can notice. Hearing is happening. Seeing is happening. Breathing is happening. The heart is beating, blood is flowing, and food is being digested. Thoughts are arising and disappearing. Life functions perfectly and effortlessly.

All Life unfolds perfectly ... without any controlling entity called "you."

But there is seemingly a sense of a "you," isn't there? What IS this "you" that comes up as a thought, like a voice-over, running alongside or on top of what simply is?

We say, "I See." Yet, have a look and notice ... the thought "I" cannot see. SEEING IS. No "I" is needed for seeing. Same for hearing; the thought "I" cannot hear. The idea of a "person," an individual "I" or "Me," is nothing but a wave of energy forming into a thought. A subtle sound. Trace that sound back to its source ... find the fountainhead. I suggest you look until you find that source; don't give up until you have got down all the way to That Emptiness from which the "I" thought arises. When you do, you'll pull the plug on suffering!

You see, in Reality, this person is an empty meaningless phantom character starring in a thought-story without substance or form: Thoughts are utterly insubstantial. And, if there is no awareness of presence, can any thought even arise? No. And without awareness-presence, the thought "I" cannot form.

Perfect Peace

When you are in dreamless sleep at night there is no "I." Yet the Awareness-Being IS. That beats the heart, That flows the blood, That breathes in and out. So clearly living is simply happening, absolutely independent of "the thinker" and the thoughts of "Me myself and I."

So what does that say about who you REALLY are?

Have a look ... If awareness is prime - and without awareness there is no Beingness, no Consciousness, no world and certainly no thought of a "me" - then what are you? Clearly ... Awareness. Just that. Knowing this is natural and spontaneous ... and ends the spiritual seeking once and for good!

Ultimately as we noted before the search for "liberation" is absolutely futile and hopeless ... because, there is no such thing! And no one to attain it. It's a story told by a seeker ... and the seeker itself is part of the story. So obviously no "person" gets liberated ... simply because in Reality there is NO person.

But don't believe or accept anything "on faith!" Investigate, using the pointers in this book, and see for yourself: You are presence-awareness, undeniable and constantly "on." You are not a thought or feeling of a separate me. Look for that "me" and prove to yourself, there is no such thing!

All there is, is Consciousness, Presence-Awareness, "I AM-ness, Aliveness ... whatever label you like to point to That which cannot be known or described, yet IS That which we ARE. This Presence is the simplicity of what is ... all there is, is This. Nothing is needed, you are already whole and complete ... as you are and as you are not.

So allow yourself to be taken over by what you are ... Natural Being-Knowing-Loving. Stop now and be as you are.

Perfect Peace

Being Is All There Is

Six: Be Nothing, Know Nothing

You have probably at least glimpsed by now that what is being pointed to here in this book is your own perfectly natural, ordinary, knowing that you are, presence-awareness. And that what you are not is a suffering separate limited fearful little "person" filled with insecurities, anxieties, and frustrations. To make this absolutely clear may take some rigorous work, and earnestness, on your part, if you are to "own" this clear Understanding - in a manner of speaking; in actual fact no one owns anything, but as we pointed out earlier in the paradox of being a "seeker" we use words and concepts to point toward That which is Nameless, Formless, Timeless ... the Being that we are.

Se let's get cracking, OK? Here are a few more points to consider...

"Who Am I Anyway? Am I my Resume?" - *A Chorus Line, Broadway musical*

What if the great I Am, the sense of a person, a me, is just a thought-story? Just a *thought of a separate* "I" ... with an add-on ... I Am ... and more added on ... I Am Me!?

What is all that in Reality? Apart from an idea, a thought, self-imagination ... is there a real, separate "me?"

Without a thought story, I still exist. I don't have to THINK I Am to BE. I cannot *NOT BE*! I DO exist... obviously! But as what? Who or what is this me that exists, and seeks a blissful state of freedom?

Am I what the sages refer to as Self Shining, Non Conceptual, Ever Fresh, Presence-Awareness? Just This and Nothing else?

If I say, yes, I am That, who is claiming this understanding as a personal attainment? Who is this person who wants freedom, peace, and happiness? Where is it? What is it made of? Is it real? Or imaginary? What is this Me, Myself, this I?

WHO is asking the questions?

Let's play hardball:

What if... every single thing you know and believe yourself to be, is NOT what you are? Do you assume facts not in evidence about the "me" you think of as yourself? What if your assumptions are based on false premises? What is a false premise? An assumption that a thing is true in the absence of investigation to look for evidence. For example, a discussion about the characteristics of the wife and children of the man in the moon assumes the existence of a phantom, a myth, a believed tale that "There IS a man in the moon." So what will WORK to stay out of the pitfalls of the mind's assumptions?

Perfect Peace

I Am

I Am the Witness; I Am the blue light in the Void.
Still I remain different from everything.
When the sight turns inward, hear what it beholds:
The inner eyes see what lies beyond the mind;
then I experience my Attributeless being.
Jnanadev says, Nivritti [the Guru] gave the Wisdom
in which I saw the whole universe within myself.

- Sri Jnaneshswar Maharaj

Seven: What WORKS?

1. Giving up knowing. This is essential for the pointers to take hold within your Being. Give up that you know anything at all. Especially anything about spirituality. Don't refuse to do this. Your openness is essential. The pointers cannot enter a closed mind-system, so believing or thinking you already know or understand what is being offered is the surest way to rip yourself off. Don't do that to yourself. We are up to ending suffering. Let's not sell out the diamond in your heart for the peanuts of stale concepts or memories or beliefs. OK?

2. Don't dismiss anything you come across here without a thorough investigation for yourself. As a wise man, Herbert Spencer, said, "There is a principle which is a bar against all information, which is proof

against all arguments and which cannot fail to keep a man in everlasting ignorance--that principle is contempt prior to investigation."

To reject a premise or a pointer out of hand is real ignorance. Don't fall for the mind's assertions that it knows what is being said or pointed out. The answer is NOT in the mind!

3. Be willing to discover you have been wrong about what you know yourself to be and what you know to be real. This book is about moving from the unreal to the real. The discovery of your True Nature will rock your world in a good way, so just let go as best you can, and LOOK from the spaces that are pointed out into your own aware presence.

4. Look at what the pointer is pointing at, not at the pointer. Judging and evaluating the pointers, forming opinions about them, and memorizing the words will all result in a failure to see the space being pointed out. Don't be like the pet cat. If you point out the window, the cat will stare at your finger. It takes courage and commitment to forgo our infinite

wisdom and look through brand new eyes at what is. ALL assumptions and beliefs MUST be challenged. Let the challenge take you over, drop the resistance, as best you can.

5. A note regarding so-called Advaita or Neo-Advaita spiritual teachings: If you have been exposed to any of that you will really need to drop them ALL ... all your cherished spiritual concepts must come under fire. Let it happen. Notice if you are hanging on to any belief – for example, "there is no person who can do anything, so I must not read and look at this", is a popular one in some circles.

"There is NO person" as a pointer, is fine. But as a belief that limits us, that belief *itself* will almost assuredly ensure that suffering continues!

Ask yourself: Would you rather be right about what you believe and know, OR would you prefer the suffering be stopped in its tracks once and for good?

OK, are you set to go?

These next few minutes could be the most important minutes of your life, if you take on what is on offer here.

I wish the end of suffering for YOU ... right here, right now.

(Suffering is defined here as the idea that what IS "should" be better, different, more, less that exactly what IS as it is. These "shoulds" are the signal that there is a secondary ego-involvement that overlays what is - and THIS is the root of all suffering.)

Eight: Who Or What Are You?

Who do you know yourself to be? Thoughts added on to I Am will come up: I Am a man, I am a consultant, I am divorced, I am etc ... look at the whole list and than just DROP all of that, and now LOOK:

Do you exist? Are you aware? You know you are, existing and aware, before you think about it. Right? Stop here and NOW. Before there is a thought "I Am" there IS the beingness. Right? Can you see that you always exist and are aware? Before time, before thought, You Are.

Look around the space you are in. Notice what is there in the space. Now notice that the awareness that knows each object in your space is always the same awareness. Look around again and notice; all the objects in your space arise IN that unchanging awareness. They are seen and known BEFORE the mind appends a label to them.

So LOOK and SEE ... What is your True Nature? What are the sages referring to as your True Self? Just This: You exist and you are aware. What you sought and needed to know was only ever that.

You ARE That... Non-Dual Presence-Awareness. Period.

That is IT. The BIG "IT" is just this simple awareness of Being ... I Am. That I Am that I Am is the same I Am that YOU are, and all the sages from Christ to Buddha, Lao Tzu to all the Zen Masters, St. John of the Cross and Ramana Maharshi and Sri Nisargadatta Maharaj ... all were the I AM that YOU are. THERE IS NO DIFFERENCE BETWEEN YOU AND A BUDDHA or a Christ. None. You are the very same Being-Awareness-Presence that everyone is. The difference is most don't know that, because they are hypnotized into believing thoughts like "I think therefore I am" or other ideas ... IDEAS ONLY ... that claim to create a separate entity where none exists.

All down through the ages the sages have declared, That I Am, IS That Thou Art. They have repeated over and over, you already ARE what you seek. You are like a fish in the ocean seeking for water.

Let's look again at this pointer: Do you doubt that you exist? And that you are aware? No one can deny the fact of his or her own existence. This simple always present Awareness of Being IS what has been sought. It is so simple.... That is always here now, was never missing, just overlooked.

That is all that is needed ... simply looking in your own actual direct experience, you cannot say I Am Not. You have to BE before anything can be said or thought. If you are not BEING then nothing else is either.

Perfect Peace

> *"The world is an out-picturing of your very own Consciousness"*
>
> - a Hindu Text

So you see, this Being that you are IS the undeniable Presence of YOU as That non-conceptual non-thought, I AM. It follows then that your Being is REQUIRED for the world to be. The manifestation does not exist without your being-awareness. You can verify this easily: When you awake from deep sleep, you as the "I Am" and the world all appear simultaneously. This appearance cannot happen unless YOU are there (here) ... BE-Ing.

Too simple? Yes ... for the mind-intellect.

The more you try to figure this out the more frustrated you will become. Because, THE ANSWER IS NOT IN THE MIND.

The mind divides up Oneness onto manyness, and it itself is an object that is a product of that energy of dividing. The mind can NEVER understand unicity; for the mind, "unity is plural and at minimum two" (as Buckminster Fuller described it.) Unicity is NOT Two ... indivisible, One-Without-A-Second, beginningless, endless, timeless, spaceless.

Simplicity itself. Got it? Reread these pointers and look into nothing from nowhere, until you are dead certain that yes, you exist and are aware, and that that existence-awareness is your own natural state of being, and that awareness has no borders, no center, no beginning, no end.

Ask yourself, Where does now begin? Where does this Beingness begin? Or end? It doesn't. See right now from this that Being is timeless and spaceless, it is the pure Consciousness, the Absolute One-Subject-Presencing ... don't stop till this is seen. You may notice doubts arise. Fine. What do they arise within? Awareness. Thoughts, feelings like "I don't get this" ... OK, where do the thoughts and feelings arise? In that Awareness.

Who do these doubting thoughts arise for? "Me." Who IS that "me?" Where is it? Track back to the

Source of the "me-myself-I" thought. Find out: Is it real? Substantial? Or is there a phantom in my soap opera? Any problem seeing that before anything can exist there must be that existence-awareness? Trust the pointers... they work.

In summary: What You ARE Is NON conceptual I AM-Ness, Presence-Awareness, Being, always fresh, self knowing and self shining, One-without-A-Second, Intelligence-Energy-Cognizing-Emptiness ... Timeless BEING. Just That.

Got it? (Who got it?)

Are you starting to see that there is really no "you" to "get" any "it?" Or NOT? Yes?

> *"The wise man does not strive for anything, not even for Dharma [good conduct and righteousness, etc.] or liberation. He is free from all actions and movements, and also from desire and renunciation."*
>
> *– The Avadhut Gita*

Nine: What You Are NOT

The thought "I" is benign and powerless.

Just a thought.

There IS The thought I ... But as that thought YOU?

Nothing that can change can be the presence-awareness, the timeless being, which you are. You have at least glimpsed this by now, yes?

Have you noticed ... this "I" thought is not always there? It is a fleeting, impermanent thought form that comes and goes. Remember the last time you were driving, and noticed that there was no thought "I am driving?" There was just ... driving, happening?

So the "Driver" is sometimes there, sometimes not. Yet the driving happens perfectly whether "you" are there or not. Stop now and see this.

Then you can look deeper ... who is driving the car REALLY? And who is driving the so-called "driver?" Take a good look: What is in control of the machine ("you") that is driving the machine ("car?") Can you find any entity? Or is it all just ... thoughts? And thoughts come and go. They are not eternal, not real, not lasting. And nothing that comes and goes can be the Real.

One basic premise needs to be kept "on screen:" Nothing that comes and goes can be Real. Or to say it another way, ONLY that which never changes can be Real.

So ... What is the thought "I" ... in Reality?

A pointer. To what?
Nothing. No Thing. Space. Awareness ... without a subject/object "relationship." The NON-Conceptual I Am ... Beingness, just That.

Perfect Peace

A Relative I says I am / You Are. Two-ness.

An Absolute I says I Am nothing. Silent Stillness Appearing as No Thing.

An Absolute I says I Am Everything. Silent Stillness Appearing As Everything.

Oneness.

'Words cannot describe this Consciousness Absolute. The mind is lost in its majesty.' – *the Avadhut Gita*

Form is Emptiness. Emptiness is Form. These are Not Two....

Not comprehensible by a mind. Absolute Paradox. Mystery. Words are futile to say it. This cannot be said.
  Yet we say this. I AM is the pointer to I. I is the pointer to No I. Or Universal I. The One I ... Love
  That separate "Me" ... in clear seeing ... is seen to be NON-existent. This investigation is NOT a mental

"process" however. This investigation is simply LOOKING. Not "Thinking About."

This "looking" is NOT a mental exercise. There are no teachings or mantras or meditations or contemplations or any other "practice." This is about a natural, easy, affectionate looking, very much the same as seeing happens through your eyes as you drive along and a beautiful seascape is noticed.

The seascape is embraced naturally by the seeing, and no "personal se-er" is needed. The "I" is redundant; all labeling by the mind is redundant.

Direct experience of looking will prove ... beyond ANY doubt ...that this separate I "entity" is simply ... ABSENT. NON-EXISTENT.

The I THOUGHT then may reassert itself and CLAIM ITS OWN ABSENCE ("I Am Nobody!") But that too is Oneness playing the great game of hide and seek with Oneness. And once these pointers take hold you can no longer buy into the lies the mind seemingly serves up.

Perfect Peace

> *"That which is false troubles the heart, but truth brings joyous tranquility."*
>
> -Rumi

This is all a Play of Consciousness.

Oneness ... nothing is really wrong or right unless thinking happens to say so...It is clear here that ALL suffering is nothing more complex that an unexamined belief in a separate I ...

Looking dissolves it and all there is, is:

Aliveness.

Paradoxically. In LOOKING there is SEEING. But there is NO ONE LOOKING and NO ONE SEEING. You see? :-))

Perfect Peace

Being Is All There Is

Thoughts arise

in Being -

AS Being -

like clouds

floating

in

Empty Space

Ten: Any When But Now?

Consider ... The eye cannot see itself... Oneness can NOT see or know Oneness ... it IS Oneness ... and That Thou Art. To paraphrase Adi Shankara, all distinctions are ultimately false. Neti Neti. (Not That Not That!) Then what is left? Nothing. Then even THAT goes, and all is Oneness, not-knowing in Divine Presence. All is That One and since you exist, you are that ... and NOT any separate character. NOT.

Somewhen around the age of two or three, a strange kind of hypnosis arose in virtually every human organism: The idea that "I" am separate and apart from Others and The World. It began in innocence ... mother said, you are Charles, I am mother, and right away separateness as a mental construct was born. The PURE I Am that we always were became polluted, so to say, by the thought ... the THOUGHT ONLY ... That I am a thing called I and added to that, I am a boy, I am ME, sister and mother are not me but other, I am alone, something is wrong, how will I survive? All added on to this core idea of a discrete "me."

Now we are at the crux of the matter of all psychological suffering: The unexamined BELIEF in the concept, the thought "I" or "Me". It was pointed out to me by Bob and other friends that this root idea is the source and cause of separation, and the idea and assumption of the actuality of a separate entity called "me" IS the root of all psychological suffering. I looked into this, thoroughly ... and became convinced due to my own investigation that there simply is no such entity as "me." And in fact there never was! It... this "me" or "I" sense ... is just an imaginary character appearing in the aliveness of the non-dual presence-awareness ... That I Am that IS, before the mind translates that Pure Consciousness into the THOUGHT I Am.

It's SO Simple.

Look: If this "me" is nothing but a thought, an idea, where is the problem if the idea is challenged? Do you "believe in me?" Let's challenge that belief, OK?

If there really is a separate real "me" in the organism we will no doubt be able to find it. So let's go on the hunt for the "me." Where is it? Look inside right now. What is the nature and essence of this "Me" idea? Can you find anything in you that you can say is YOU beyond doubt? Is there anything in there with ANY independent nature or substance, apart from a thought arising presently in the Awareness that you now know yourself to BE?

This bears repeating: See if there is really a separate "me" that can suffer ... is there a "person" in the organism? Isn't the idea of "me" just a *thought*? Who is thinking? Who is looking? Some investigation reveals that the separate person is completely non-existent. Seeing the unreal nature of the "me" allows for an immediate end to psychological suffering.

With some looking, it is seen that awareness is present and the separate person is absent. Seeing this is not a mental construct. The answer is NOT in the mind! It is a clear knowing without words or anything else. It just IS. Inescapable and undeniable.

What you ARE is Presence-Awareness ... Being, Just That.

What you are NOT is a separate entity. The "me" is a phantom.

And That is That.

This communication is from Self to Self. There is no "Charlie" or "You." All there is, is Consciousness.

This is IT.

> "*It is due to illusion born of ignorance that men fail to recognize That which is always and for everybody the inherent Reality dwelling in its natural Heart-center and to abide in it, and that instead they argue that it exists or does not exist, that it has form or has not form, or is non-dual or dual.*"

– Sri Ramana Maharshi,
"Forty Verses on Reality, v 34.

In clear seeing these are distinct: Consciousness as all that appears - and the Absolute, the One-that-cannot-be-seen-or-known - then it collapse into Not Two. I love the pointer, "the eye cannot see itself" - just as the Pure-I-Oneness, cannot see or know itSelf. All knowing requires a split into knower/known ... the mind is that Energy Intelligence splitting one into two-and many and all ... as a pseudo subject... a false authoring entity ... the great Divine Trickster. All appearing in the Absolute non-dual Isness...

Know that you are presence awareness. Know that you are NOT a separate "person." See the falseness of the idea of "me" once and for good. Then the suffering cannot arise and (seemingly) overshadow what you are.

~

The beautiful form of The beloved
has settled in these eyes.
There is no room left for any other beauty.

- Rahim

Perfect Peace

Eleven: Suffering Ends NOW

Follow along with this and put yourself in the picture. You will notice how simple the end of suffering actually is!

All "my worries" ... about money, health, ending up homeless unless I find work, getting old, feeling insecure and vulnerable, and so alone ... all that *only* arise in thinking ... and as "Sailor" Bob Adamson notes in the title of his book - "What's wrong with Right Now, unless you think about it?"

Clearly, none of that exists in the Awareness, the *non conceptual I Am-ness* ... here and now. Only in thinking there is a real, separate "me" can there be worries about a non-existent future. Pure imagination. I SEEM to have an imaginary person in "my" mind ... me. But when I look ... right now ... to try to find this "me" I come up empty. It is just a thought! Like a cloud, it has no actual substance!

Another question from "Sailor" Bob Adamson sheds light: "Who needs to know HOW?" (to make life work...)

Go on the hunt for that "one" and you will never find it! Why? It does not exist. Did you need to know "how" to grow the body from the single sperm cell and ovum? Was there a "you" that thought, "I am the sperm cell" and did that "you" know "how" to "find the ovum, and join with it?" And "attach yourself to the wall of the uterus?"

Come on: A little solid investigation and the whole house of cards collapses! All that is happening is JUST HAPPENING ... as the perfect and divine functioning of the Energy-Intelligence that is the unseen substance of all that appears to be.

And what about "time?" Is there any when outside of now? Any where outside of here? Who knows this? Or NOT? Who am I?

Now ask ... Who is asking these questions?

(Silence.)

"What's wrong with Right Now ... unless you think about it?"

-"Sailor" Bob Adamson

The sages point out that any separate "Me" apart from presence-awareness ... in clear seeing through thorough investigation ... is simply NON existent. They say this investigation is NOT a mental "process" however.

This investigation is simply LOOKING. Not "Thinking About." Looking non-conceptually ... inquiring within. Am I really separate from awareness and others? My body is separate from other bodies; at least it seems so ... but what if that is just another thought attached to the "I" ... I Am my body in a world...?

Really? Is that true? The MIND-Story says, "I think so. I believe so. "

Where is this thinking, believing, knowing? Language. All words pinned to the core belief in a separate "I" ... thoughts.

Without a thought who am I?

Who am I?

Who is asking the question?

Your own direct experience of looking will show you that this separate I "entity" is simply ... ABSENT. NON-EXISTENT. The "I" story, all the feelings and words and pictures, which has been repeated for decade after decade, then reasserts itself, and "I" am back in the soup! Until it is seen clearly that what I am is this: I exist. I am aware. That is always present, being is never missing, and all the "me" stories that arise and subside do so IN that space of Being-Awareness.

So where is the problem?

It's gone in a flash of seeing. Awareness, just that, is what I Am. All else is an appearance in that and has no existence apart from that! Suffering is nothing more complex than an unexamined belief in a separate I ... an entity separate from Presence. On investigation this 'entity' is seen to be nothing more than a will o' the wisp ... a phantom made of energy, letters, words ... all imaginary.

The ghost is not real.

A little looking and there it is ...

Realize! "What I am is Being, just that ... Presence-Awareness. What I am not is a separate personal being-entity. Perfect Peace. <u>This</u> is the end of suffering."

Perfect Peace

All there is is Being

Being As-It-Is

Being Is All There Is

There Is Nothing That Is Not Being.

Who thinks this is not true?
who thinks this IS true?

Turn Around Now!

Find that One and the search is over.

Twelve: Suffering is About a "me"

And there isn't any such thing!

Note: Some pointers are repeated throughout this text, for the simple reason that repetition works. This chapter contains some of that; I suggest you read it as though you have never seen or heard anything on the page before. Then the pointers can do their work.

Have you noticed? Any and all problems ... financial, health, love life, situations like career or work, family ... are always and only for the mythical imaginary person called me, myself and I?

Looking directly into what we call life and living, isn't it obvious that all so called troubles consist in thoughts and emotions, body sensations and feelings?

Is there inherently anything wrong with all that? When there is the clarity that what you are is Presence, Awareness, Being, Consciousness - whichever label you like - then these thoughts and feelings and sensations, whether pleasurable or painful, simply are appearances in the empty sky of what you actually are.

But if there is a subtle sense that what is happening, is happening to "ME", well, then all that becomes suffering ... "I am hurting and I want it to stop" or "I am in bliss and I want it to stay" are equally problematic when there is that imagination that "I am separate from everything else and this is happening to ME."

What is the antidote to suffering?

It is startlingly simple:

Perfect Peace

First, understand what you are: Do you exist? Are you aware? That simple awareness of being is "IT" ... your true nature. It is just that simple. Seeking anything beyond this is just the mind wanting more or better, something more spectacular. Just know that what you are is this ordinary being-awareness and at the same time know that any "more" or "better" or "different" is only imaginary mind stuff and NOT what you are!

Then stop, and see, the answer is NOT in the mind! You already ARE what you sought in meditation, chanting, sitting, doing service, and making endless pilgrimages to Satsangs and gurus and all that. JUST STOP. You are ALREADY what you sought.

Presence-Awareness. Just That.

Now, looking within the space of awareness, see if you can find any separate entity, any "me" as a real, substantial object ...apart from a thought or idea of an I or a me or a sense, a feeling. Is that sense or feeling what you actually are? NO. See this right now and suffering is over. It is only the belief in separation that causes suffering. Root out that belief by looking, investigating.

Don't dismiss the possibility without looking for yourself. This is NOT a philosophical matter; it is a practical, hard hitting way to see for yourself what the cause of suffering is, and root it out once and for all. The me thought has NO substance or independent existence apart from the steadily self-shining awareness it arises within ... and in looking closely at that "me sense" it is seen for what it is ... A PHANTOM, an ephemeral, imagined self center that never actually existed at all!

> *"Actions happen, deed are done, but there is NO individual 'doer' thereof"*
>
> – The Buddha

Thirteen: Suffering Is Distinct From Pain

Suffering is Optional.

Suffering and pain are different. How? Basically, pain is a signal that something is not working in the organism. Dogs have pain. Humans have pain. But the dog does not suffer... because the dog does not have a sense of being a separate entity that takes ownership of the pain and adds the secondary idea that the pain "should not be."

The sage Nisargadatta Maharaj pointed to this perfectly. Late in his life his body was wracked with pain from Cancer. One time a visitor asked him as he saw him wincing, "Maharaj, are you in great pain?"

The sage replied, "There IS great pain." This is illuminating when looked into. There IS great pain, acknowledges a condition of the body but makes no claim to owning that pain. In Presence-Awareness, anything can arise. But it is NOT "taken on board."

All that arises is simply what IS ... and is not a personal matter. Once it is seen that what we ARE is Presence-Awareness and what we are NOT is "an individual" the game is over; you can no longer believe that pain is personal, any more than you can believe the earth is flat.

It may take some deep looking for this to be seen ... especially if there is severe pain. For example, being wracked by spasms of coughing may seem to take the attention so completely to the body that the awareness appears to have been "forgotten." But in actual fact is the awareness ever really missing? No. It cannot be.

So possibly what is needed in these instances is to look, as soon as possible, into what it is that is in pain or suffering about there being a wracking cough.

We say or think, "I am coughing. I am in pain." We add on to the awareness "I Am" and say I Am in pain. Making a sharp distinction between this "I Am awareness and that which has pain ... the body-mind organism ... does the trick. When the sword of razor sharp discrimination is brought to bear on this business of the thought story "I am in pain" then it is seen ... effortlessly ... that FIRST is I. *this PURE I* is just Awareness. Oneness. I-I, as the sage Ramana Maharshi referred to it. Then next comes I AM ... Awareness, arising as Consciousness. Pure knowingness, no subject-object split ... just the knowing Existence Is and I Am That.

THEN comes the mischief made of the thought machinery ... the mind. The MIND says I Am this BODY, and that is taken on board by the I Am as a belief in something real called "my body."

That's the trigger for suffering, as the mind adds on, I am in pain, I don't like that, I want that to change, why is this happening to me ....

Poor me! Etc.

Notice that all this is pinned to a core belief in the identification with the body! And yet, where is the body except in a thought story appearing presently?

Making the distinction (notional only, a concept that *may* remove a false concept that is unseen!) between the pure I Am, Awareness-Presence, and the thoughts that arise IN that Awareness, makes all the difference in seeing that while there may well be pain for one who has seen his or her True Nature, there is NO suffering, because suffering is only possible for the fictional person, and once that "person" has been seen to be nothing more than thoughts, based on a belief in a separate "me" thing identified as a body with a name etc., the game is over.

Once you know that the earth is round you no longer buy into the story that you dare not sail out too far or you'll fall off ... once you know beyond doubt that the phantom is a ghost and is not real you cannot put the energy of belief into that phantom and its stories any longer.

The end of suffering is simple: Investigate who sees, who thinks, who you are, and see the false nature of the "one who suffers." Then remain as you are ... Presence-Awareness, just that. Simple and natural. Home.

"The observed, observation and observer are mental constructs. The Self alone is." –*Sri Nisargadatta Maharaj*

The ever-fresh non-conceptual ... That which is registering these very words ... is "IT." In seeing this, the suffering ends ... even if there is pain in the organism (I say from direct experience.)

And the word "IT" is another concept! Language must end in the true seeing of "IT" ... there IS no "IT. IT is just a word. Like in "It's a nice day."

What is the IT? Not one single or manifold thing. NO thing cannot be expressed in language, which is itself a thing!

WHO does not "see" or Get" this?

These words and images and spaces on the page are only pointers to IT. The one who understands is it. The one who does NOT understand is it. The separation and dualism of that separateness is it.

The Unicity of all things is it.

Seeker: "I am SO angry! This thing happened and I got SO angry - I am SO upset. I don't WANT to be so ANGRY? Help me please O Guru!

<u>Guru</u>: There is no anger. Being is Being Energy Being labeling itself anger. WHO wants to NOT be Being? Anger is Being. That Thou Art. Who wants anything other than what is? You?

WHO are YOU? WHO?

Find Out.

Fourteen: Is Anything NOT "IT?"

Nothing <u>is</u> "It."

<u>Not</u> the *word* nothing. The word is never the actual! Try to get a bucket of "blue" water out of the ocean. Or drink the word "water."

EVERYTHING is IT. This is the Mystery. This text is all simply pointing the actually non-existent yet perhaps still accepted as real "you" back to your Eternal Essence.

You *are* that impersonal empty awareness that sees and hears, AND all that appears within That. You have never *not* been That!

All there is and ever was or will be is That.

"That" is the Eternal unknowable yet undeniable Presence-Awareness. Arising as Consciousness and all the objects in Consciousness ... all an appearance of the essence of no thing as objects. To paraphrase a dear friend, John Greven, Any reflection in a mirror is ONLY a reflection and not the mirror. Even when that reflection is nothing.

Look. Right Now.

Are YOU thinking? Or do thoughts simply arise in the awareness?

Do the eyes see? Do the ears hear? Or is there a seeing happening THROUGH the eyes, hearing THROUGH the ears?

Thoughts are arising in the Space. Notice this. Just stop and look.

The One you have been looking for is the One who is LOOKING.

Right now, this very instant-before-time.

You are that.

And that is an ocean of awareness-love-freedom.

Pure naked possibility -

arising as Unbounded LOVE.

Salutations to You from in front and behind, salutations to You on all sides, O God of All.

You are infinite courage and boundless might.

You pervade all, therefore, You are All.

- The Bhagavad Gita

Fifteen: End Game

As the energy of false belief and the false believer (the "I") no longer is fed to these thought forms, they just fade away into the Cognizing Emptiness. They just die as any unfed "thing" dies.

No energy, no life. Have you noticed? Unfed bodies die eventually. All "things" come only to pass ... not to stay. All that stays is no thing / every thing.

The Absolute alone (all one) IS.

That arises AS Aliveness, which manifests as all there is, including the ideas of separation and completeness, endarkenment and enlightenment ... everything.

Unicity. That alone IS. This cannot be known ... it is no more possible for any "one" (which requires the existence of the concept "other") to know That, than it is for the eye to see itself or the ear to hear itself, as all there is, IS That.

Period.

Tat Tvam Asi. Perfect Peace.

A Sage once said,

"If a Human Being does not find his True Nature, he has sold a diamond for the price of spinach."

But, get it or not, know it or not, YOU ARE THAT.

Period. Finished. Done.

Stop.

Sixteen: An Ego's Last Stand

The last stand of the ego-mind is found in the zeal for the co-opting of the fact of Being No Thing into someone who OWNS that ... thereby seemingly becoming "somebody who knows they are nothing."

This is the trap of the fabled "enlightened ego." The claim by an entity that there is no entity!

There can be great intellectual "clarity" about what is real and what is unreal ... but as long as "Someone" OWNS that "clarity" then you can be sure that the Final Truth has not revealed itself. Because this Understanding IS NOT A PERSONAL MATTER. This cannot be stressed too much ... a

Perfect Peace

common pitfall in the unfolding of non-duality is this notion that "Aha! Now I am enlightened." One does not have to look far to see Satsang teachers claiming this enlightenment and offering to "teach" others "how to get enlightened."

That is spiritual arrogance. How can anyone teach you to BE? It would be as though I was claiming to be able to teach you how to beat your heart and digest your food. It's utter nonsense at best and an often-expensive con game at worst.

You ARE. THAT is indisputable! If there are vestiges of identification with the body or mind, with thoughts or feelings, then BE YOUR OWN GURU. Look within. Inquire: Who Am I?

Don't stop until you see beyond ANY doubt that the thought-form "I" is a FALSE entity. The "I" thought is NOT real. It has no existence apart from the Awareness that you are. If identification seems to persist, keep looking for the SOURCE of the I-thought. From where does it arise? What is its substance? Does it have any independent nature apart from the Awareness that you are? Does it have any mass or shape? Doesn't it come and go? And can anything that comes and goes be ultimately real?

No.

Who Am I? ASK!

This is not a "mantra" to be repeated, but rather an effortless looking into the Space-Like Awareness with a natural curiosity, devoid of preconceptions or answers, with innocence and no agenda. You are not looking for an outcome! It is merely an objective investigation, like looking into the innards of a clock to see what makes it tick.

Then allow the pointer to arise:

"Who is asking 'Who am I?'"

This investigation happens naturally when the zeal to find "the right answer" is forsworn and the looking is just a simple peering into the space, as one might peer into a dimly lit room to see what is there.

Perfect Peace

Keep at it as long as there is any sense of separation left. Allow the answers to float up and disappear; don't hold to ANY answer. Answers are concepts and NOT real. They are just thoughts appearing and disappearing, devoid of substance, unreal in essence. Appearances. Phenomenon.

What IS real is Noumenon. That which cannot be known through perception, although its existence can be demonstrated... i.e. by the absolute FACT that existence unarguably IS.

Do the inquiry as long as there is ANY subtle sense left that "you" are a separate "do-er."

Discover once and for good that the I thought is as insubstantial and powerless as a cloud in the summer sky. Let the Light of Awareness shine through that cloud. Watch as it dissipates. Naturally, as your own Awareness of Presence shines as the light of pure knowing and reveals all the thought stories to be as dreams, with no power and no actual reality.

Perfect Peace

Who Am I? When there is no answer, there is no question ... and no questioner.

Who asks the question?

Then it is seen, that question and question-ER are one essence, energy forming into sounds letters words concepts. And YOU are not that.

<u>Who asks the question?</u>

And Here is the Silence that You Are.

Perfect Peace

Let nothing perturb you,
nothing frighten you.
All things pass.
God never changes.
Patience achieves everything.
Whoever has God lacks nothing.
God alone suffices.

- Teresa of Avila

Seventeen: Be Still & Know, I Am.

That.

Not Two- Not One.

Just This, As it Is.

> Take the idea "I was born". You may take it to be true. It is not. You were not born, nor will you ever die. It is the idea that was born and shall die, not you. By identifying yourself with it you became mortal."
>
> –Sri Nisargadatta Maharaj

I Am That I Am

There is Only ONE I Am

That Thou Art

Perfect Peace

Eighteen: Looking For The Keys

Once upon a time there was a fellow who lost his house keys. He was frantically searching for them under the street light, in the overgrown brush, digging and perspiring. He had been at it for more than a half hour when a neighbor, out for a stroll, happened onto the scene.

"What are you searching for, my friend?" The neighbor inquired.

"My house keys! I can't get in my house and I am so tired and I have an early appointment! It is so frustrating!" The kindly neighbor knelt down and said, "Here, I will help you look for them." After both dug around for a few minutes to no avail, the neighbor asked, "Do you recall, about where did you drop the keys?"

The hapless fellow replied, "Oh, I lost them over there by the door to the house. But you see, there is no LIGHT over there!"

We are like the seeker of the keys in that we seek the Peace of Being-Awareness where it isn't ... in the MIND. There are no answers (or endless answers and endless questions if you prefer) in the "thinking machine" we call "the mind."

Looking in the apparent light for the Self that IS our True Nature is very much like looking for the keys where they are not just because there is some seeming light there. But the light of the "mind" is actually darkness, compared to the brightly shining Light of the undeniable Presence-Awareness IN WHICH - and AS an ASPECT OF - the thought-feeling-story ARISES. The moral of the story is, Right NOW; just stop looking for the Self where it isn't!

Nineteen: What Am I Missing?

On being a 'pissed off person'

<u>Questioner:</u> *I have seen the Promised Land! That is I have clearly seen that Awareness or Presence, or Awareness of Presence as Bob Adamson puts it, IS what I am and that is all I am in truth. BUT, I still get into battles with what is on almost a daily basis and it hurts me. I feel I am still missing something crucial in all this. I've read a lot of books, and been meditating for over 23 years, and it's really been getting me down lately, all this upset and anger still coming up and feeling I will never really be free. I know all this "comes up in presence" but knowing that just doesn't cut it when I am in traffic, late for an*

appointment, and frustrated, feeling road rage at all the stupid drivers and the lousy directions the guy gave me that got me lost on the way - then I lash out and blame traffic, the guy, and myself.

Blame still happens and it is so fast I can't seem to catch it in time to keep my focus on awareness like you guys are saying is the ticket, because I get hooked and man I am gone into the upset and it runs on and on, sometimes for like an hour. Then after I calm down it is clear again that not only is awareness all I am now, all of that was also a story with a lot of emotion and loud noise coming up in awareness. But I am so sick and tired of going into that temper-tantrum and screaming curses at the top of my voice in my car at the world which just refuses to bend to my will. I understand that I'm just fighting what is – it is and it doesn't care a damn about whether I like it or not. The traffic could care less what I want.

<u>Answer</u>: It is exactly what it is – and you are right on – traffic and wrong directions and all that are what is – and it is whether "you" like it or not!

Your thinking is, "I am against What Is! I am completely against Reality." It's like arguing with gravity. Gravity doesn't care. Go out on a starry night and tell The Milky Way what you want. Tell the moon what you think ought to be different, or better. Notice the divine indifference to what we want.

The nature of a personal identity is to want. What does IT want? WHAT ISN'T. That's total insanity. We are insane as a human culture. Your generous and open expression is a great example of how the mind of humankind operates to create incredible suffering.

Q: *This keeps happening over and over and over despite the completely clear presence of the obvious fact that I am, I exist, there is the awareness before all else. But when the focus goes onto the content of awareness and I am once again a puppet being jerked around in crude and vulgar expressing I am not a bit happy about that and I want it to stop.*

A: And it will continue to happen as long as it does. It is what is appearing in the world of that body-mind thing – the puppet can only dance to the puppet masters tune. Are you pulling your own strings? Are you creating your own suffering getting all pissed off and lashing out and maybe burning bridges in the process? That's is NONE of YOUR doing. It's all being done THROUGH the puppet-you.

It's clear in what you (so generously) share that there is some homework to be done. Perhaps Grace will create a deep inquiry for you into who or what believes that you are doing any of this. Who is it the believes "I am a pissed off person?"

Or that a "you" can change your resistance to What Is? Grace leads us to inquiry - perhaps. No promises.

It may be that - if this suffering day you had is sufficient call for you to take on the investigation into what it is that is the root of all this painful behavior - you may begin to sense the unassailable permanence of that freedom that you have glimpsed – that is, the Awareness which is never actually absent – as you say yourself, you do understand that Awareness is the True State. What appears to be happening in the play is that simply your attention is not sufficiently rooted in the Present awareness of being that there seems – ONLY seems – to be a "going in and out of that."

Q: Any advice for me? I'd really appreciate any help you can offer, Charlie.

A: There are a couple of "approaches" to all this you might – if Grace leads you to – experiment with. First off, you already have accepted, at least conceptually, that Awareness is Prime and never really absent.

Secondly, you see that all these tantrums and bad feelings and emotions and lashing out come to pass – not to stay. Let's start with the simplicity of the pointer that NOTHING that changes can be the actual Eternal State. Only That which never changes – simple Awareness itself – can be the Eternal, the real. Focus on That – Awareness – rather than the content of Awareness.

Finally, consider that ALL that is going on in the focusing on content and "getting lost in it" is due to a MISTAKE – fundamental, perhaps deeply ingrained so to say – but nevertheless simply an error. "What we have here, my dear Sherlock, is a case of mistaken identity."

We have been conditioned virtually since birth to believe "I am a person." This false belief arises - from where we do not know - at an early age – I watch my 11-month-old granddaughter already pound here tiny fist on the table if she is not allowed to have a shiny and attractive (to her) object that is dangerous, like a knife, as her mother pulls it away. She's clearly pissed off and wants it period and pounds a little fist in frustration when she can't have it. That is like we are, in traffic or being late because "someone screwed up the directions." It's all blame blame blame – and it's a long- standing human habit to blame! "I want it she won't give it so I am unhappy and it's HER fault!"

All this is about a person who wants what is NOT – and it could be said about the "global" human

Perfect Peace

being as it is currently configured – "I Want Therefore I Am." Not only that, but also: "They way things work around here is, we do things MY way or I will fight, yell, kick, scream, bite – and when I grow up – throw bombs at you if you don't Gimme Gimme Gimme." Humanity – look around! - is wild, reckless, and out of control. We are along for this crazy ride – until Grace steps in inquiry is taken up.

WHO wants what isn't? Who Am I?

Meanwhile this mistake is a damn costly one – that's what I'm trying to point out. The mistake may or may not be "correctable" globally. That is nothing we can really control. But it is possible to correct the mistake locally. In US. Are you a person really? Because if there were no person there could be no upset! It's as simple as that.

Consider this from Nisargadatta Maharaj:

"There is no such thing as a person. There are only restrictions and limitations. The sum total of these defines the person. You think you know yourself when

you know <u>what</u> you are. But you never know <u>who</u> you are. The person merely appears to be, like the pot appears to have the shape and volume and spell of the pot. See that you are not what you believe yourself to be. Fight with all the strength at your disposal against the idea that you are nameable and describable. You are not. Refuse to think of yourself in terms of this or that. There is no other way out of your misery, which you have created for yourself through blind acceptance without investigation. Suffering is a call for inquiry, all pain needs investigation. Don't be lazy to think."

- "I Am That," page 204

Ask Who Am I? and let that thought burn out the false and reveal the already always Presence that you ARE.

Perfect Peace

Twenty: Self Clears Its Self

Follow-up Q: After reading over your response several times, I went to bed puzzled and still frustrated at this roller-coaster emotion of anger that I can't seem to control. But something in what you wrote hit me right where "I" live, I think – because I was not nearly as hooked in to the story of something being wrong with me because I was emotionally raging and out of control yesterday in traffic. I don't quite know how to put this in words. But the way it was last night was like this: There is a sense of a me or a being that really does never change – but it's not peaceful. It's not the accepting space I have seen pointed to by you, Bob, Tony, Annette and others. What I am trying to say is, it just still doesn't seem good enough, not like some final truth of my being.

Perfect Peace

When I woke up this morning there was a sense of freedom and deep peace, and I thought, this must be what's being pointed to as my actual what-never-changes self nature. But it passed, so I guess that wasn't the real thing either. Can I ever really know what this is that the Advaita teachings are trying to say? I am starting to think the whole thing really is hopeless, like Tony says.

Meanwhile though, I am more peaceful. I noticed this morning that something that would have set me off into impatience yesterday (a little thing, dropping something) brought almost no reaction today. So compared to yesterday it's better. Isn't this a good sign?

I am going to try to take up the inquest! What is the source of "me?" As I am looking right now, there doesn't seem to really BE any source of me. Yet that me is still absolutely here as both thought and a sense of beingness. Thought or not, there IS a me here that knows it exists.

<u>Answer:</u> Life IS. Living IS. Existence IS. There is no way that can be doubted. But what can be

doubted and questioned is the background assumption that this existence is "my" existence. Are you actually apart from me in essence? Are you other than God or Source or Being – Diving Being, if you like that term?

Is there any separateness in reality? There IS the appearance of separate unique bodies – billions of them! But are all those bodies individual BEINGS? Or is there ONE Being with billions of forms called human beings?

You are definitely on the right track if you are starting to see that what you are is never absent – that awareness that was present when you were 3 years old is the very same awareness that is present reading these words (and present here now watching the typing of these words.) Isn't that so? Verify this right now. And if you are starting to ask the big question in all these circumstances – WHO? – WHO gets angry? Who is impatient? Who wants to NOT be impatient?

WHO,? then you are at the "end game."

Perfect Peace

Test this for yourself in daily living. This understanding of your True Nature as Being-Awareness is not of a lot of value in the cave – if it can't stand the test of being-in-the-world of day by day living with all the crap that can arrive to disturb the peace. What is ultimately the possibility being pointed out by the "sages" is that what you really ARE is at peace with whatever "war" is happening around you or even within you.

Take up this question and keep me advised on how it opens out for you:

<u>What NEVER Changes?</u>

Noticing that all states of being, all emotional states, all peace and all conflict, come to pass (NOT to stay - Thank Grace.)

ASK as much as you can remember to ask, in ALL circumstance that arise – in traffic, at lunch, in an argument with someone, in any upset AND any peaceful moment – WHAT IS IT THAT NEVER CHANGES?

Perfect Peace

However: JUST UNDERSTAND that even this - Self-Inquiry- is NOT necessarily going to "produce a result." That is hard to hear! I am suggesting these things as a means to kind of see what is real as a glimpse - but the paradox of all this is useful, as I see it, to keep present:

There is nothing you can do to gain Liberation - there's no you" who can gain anything.

The you that wants Liberation is actually NON-EXISTENT.

AND - So long as an energy of belief is going into a" me" that needs to "do" something to "get free," then we can "do inquiry."

Write back soon! Keep going – freedom is what you are – and That "wants you to come home to her right now." (Poetic nonsense - but nonetheless, a pointer!)

I Love You.

PS: Here's a bit from Nisargadatta that sheds light on the possibility of ending the seeking:

M: "Liberation is not the result of some means skillfully applied, nor of circumstances.

"It is beyond the causal process. <u>Nothing can compel it, nothing can prevent it</u>."

Q: Then why are we not free here and now?

M: "But we are free 'here and now.' It is only the mind that imagines bondage."

Q: What will put an end to imagination?

M: "Why should you want to put an end to it? Once you know your mind, and its miraculous powers, and remove what poisoned it – the idea of a separate and isolated person – you just leave it alone to do its work among things for which it is well suited.

Perfect Peace

"To keep the mind in its own place and on its own work is the liberation for the mind."

And this:

"Nothing stands in the way of your liberation and it can happen here and now, but for your being more interested in other things. And you cannot fight with your interests. You must go with them, see through them and watch them reveal themselves as mere errors of judgment..."

- I Am That, Page 456.

Perfect Peace

"The flame of love is not different from you; it is you. It isn't that love is there and you are here. You and love are one and the same."

- Gurumayi Chidvilasananda

Twenty-One: What Never Changes?

What is *That*
    which *Never*
        Changes?

    Being Is. Here Now.
      Loving to just . . . BE.
        It's Open and Inescapable.

Here - right Now - there is a sharing ...

of Aliveness.

A Vibrant One-Energy -

appearing presently - as *all that is.*

Feel This Now:

Right Here - where you ARE - there is Presence - Presencing. It's undeniable that you exist. The question is - what is it that *is aware that you exist? That* is Pure Awareness - Unknowable Unimaginable Clear Presence. *Being.* You *are* That Being. That's all there is to "enlightenment."

No bells and whistles! Just This. Beyond perception, beyond understanding, beyond conception, beyond the mind that wants to own it - It alone IS.

If you are seeking - you're knocking on the door to Paradise from INSIDE Paradise.

Twenty-Two: In The End

(Being Is All There Is.)

I have not attained some awakening or liberation or some other mythical mystical "state." I have nothing you don't have. You are the same I Am - Being - as I Am, and all the Sages and Gurus and seekers are.

We are - Simply - BEING. There is but ONE I Am. That Is IT. That is what you are.

That is all there is to express - in so many wonderful and wild ways.

Perfect Peace

This Is It.

Appendix One: Ramana

An apparent Contradictions Of Pointers

There are many seeming contradictions from various "teachers" regarding the practice or occurring of "Self-Enquiry." This page will not resolve these seeming conflicts. Resolution can only occur as an intellectual understanding of a pointer - which turns the elegant pointer into ever more spiritual bullshit.

These pointings are not REPRESENTATIONS of some knowing- some "truth." Take them for what they are - only concepts! Assigning meaning or some "authentic validity" to a concept of "Truth" is yet another story - being arising as a false conception of the un-nameable Isness of Being. The pointers are not what they seem to be. Being Is All There Is – arising as false teachers and teachings and all concepts and experiences.

That is all there is to say – and THAT is NOT TRUE EITHER!

For Example: To one seeker, Sri Ramana Maharshi - the famous Sage of Non-duality - said: "The thought 'who am I?' will destroy all other thoughts, and like the stick used for stirring the burning pyre, it will itself in the end get destroyed. Then, there will arise Self-realization."

To another, the same sage, Ramana, said: "There is no greater mystery than this: ourselves being the Reality, we seek to gain Reality. We think there is something hiding our Reality and that it must be destroyed before the Reality is gained. That is ridiculous. A day will dawn when you will yourself laugh at your past efforts. That which will be the day you laugh is also here and now."

Appendix Two: Navnath Sampradaya

Lineage Of Sri Nisargadatta Maharaj

"Your own self is your ultimate teacher (Sadguru). The outer teacher (guru) is merely a milestone. It is only your inner teacher that will walk with you to the goal, for it is the goal."

- Sri Nisargadatta Maharaj

Sri Nisargadatta Maharaj was part of the Navnath Sampradaya, the lineage of the nine Gurus, which is said to have started from the teachings of Sri Dattatreya, reputedly the teacher of Maharshi Patanjali.

Sri Dattatreya is mentioned in Markadenya Purana, and Bhagavata Purana. Sri Dattatreya is said to have composed the Avadhuta Gita and is mentioned extensively in Tripura Rahasya.

(Maharaj himself did not stress his lineage with most of his western devotees.)

Om Namo Bhagavate Nisargadatta

Many have encouraged Charlie to share his experience, and so Charlie points out the actuality of Being and shares what works, at his home, The Aspens, in Santa Ana, California, USA. He also offers Reiki Healings, and teaches Reiki as well, on request.

Charlie says:

"I know beyond doubt, that what I am IS Presence-Awareness. So are you. We were never separate at all. It was a wild and beautiful dream."

Contact and Meetings Information

Your comments, questions, and insights are most welcome... e-mail non.duality@yahoo.com.

Meetings in Absolute Freedom - Abiding As the Perfect Peace of Being - The Home You Never Left:

CALL or e-mail to arrange a meeting on the day you wish to attend. To RSVP, or to schedule a personal meeting or a telephone discussion with Charlie, call USA +1 580-701-4793 or contact non.duality@yahoo.com.

Meetings are held in Enid, Oklahoma (90 minutes from Oklahoma City, OK.)

All are welcome.

Info: "One on One"

If you would like to engage in a direct consultation to resolve doubts and questions, feel free to ask about that.

There is no set fee - but since we are a non-profit affair and depend on donations to continue The Work, donations according to your means are appreciated.

One on one consults often quickly dissolve all niggling vestiges of false belief and the never-absent True Nature is then no longer (seemingly) obscured.

E-mail charliehayes36@yahoo.com or call USA + 1-580-701-4793 for details or to set up an appointment.

Book Reviews:

"*Life After Death* is a free-wheeling spiritual romp that points directly to the Truth of who you really are...deep down. The Author blasts open the doors of misperception with his very readable and entertaining style that compels the Reader to go both onward and *inward*. In the end, Charlie succeeds brilliantly in his mission to dis-illusion the Reader from the long-standing belief in the existence of an individual and separate 'person-hood.' Highly recommended."

- *Chuck Hillig, Author* of *Enlightenment for Beginners, The Way IT Is, Seeds for the Soul, Looking for God (Seeing the Whole in One)* and *The Magic King*

"It looks like your book - '*From I Am To I Am, With Love,*' is generating some enthusiastic responses. Best of all it is bringing real benefit to people looking for answers. It is obvious that some have already benefited deeply and their doubts and suffering have been eased or eradicated. That is what it is all about. The message is clear and shared with great enthusiasm and love. Your words and example are making a positive impact. There is no doubt about it."

   - John Wheeler author of "Awakening to The Natural State", "Shining In Plain View" and "Right Here, Right Now,"

"Charlie's journey to understanding was a wild ride, and his story makes for very interesting reading. I'm so happy to see this generous expression of sharing coming so clearly and enthusiastically from someone who was a self-admitted 'tough nut to crack.'"

   - Annette Nibley, author of www.whatneverchanges.com

Perfect Peace

From I Am
to I Am
With Love

Perfect Peace

Perfect Peace

No Way Out

Question: I am angry and depressed, because I have been seeking this presence or awareness of being for damn near 25 years of practices and prayers and karma yoga and all that stuff and I am so TIRED!

And there is this guy who got it in two years, so the story goes. I beg for this! It's happened for you, right, Charlie? When will it happen for me? I am really sick of seeking yet I can't stop!

A: As to my experience or lack thereof - who cares? I don't mean that in a nasty way! I am just inviting you to ask yourself that question. WHO is in there that cares about "someone else's "attainment" or "realization?"

"Charlie" does not have the same perspective as "the guy who got it in two years" - nor anyone else.

Perfect Peace

"You" will never get this. Neither will "Charlie." Whatever happens is whatever happens - including getting or not getting ANYTHING - EVEN NO THING.

I suggest that you do whatever practice you like – or stop if you like. Chant and meditate if that is what you like. DO what you like to do. That's about all I can offer. And I am safe in suggesting this – because that's what we do anyway! T

Then if you'd like to add Self-Inquiry you can try that. But a good question right here might be – WHO meditates? WHO self-inquires? WHO chants or does "karma yoga?" WHO?

No answer is true.

All answers are in the mind.
What is being pointed to is beyond the comprehension of the mind and cannot be "owned" by it.

This message contains absolutely NO hope. All hope for a better future is bondage.

Liberation is the natural abandonment of hope – but "you" can't DO that!

Try as you might, this Presence is ungraspable and yet IT IS. It's hopeless – really. But - REALLY.

"Getting" This Brings Perfect Peace.

Perfect Peace

www.ingramcontent.com/pod-product-compliance
Lightning Source LLC
Chambersburg PA
CBHW050827160426
43192CB00010B/1923